MYSTERIES
OF THE ANCIENT WORLD

STONE
CIRCLES

AUBREY BURL

WEIDENFELD & NICOLSON
LONDON

S tonehenge is a wonder. It is also a contradiction. Its stones are high and heavy but they were pounded and shaped by woodworkers. No stones were available on Salisbury Plain, but determined to construct an enduring monument native carpenters dragged scores of massive sandstones from far

S tonehenge. Looking across the ring to the entrance and the Heel Stone.

away, up hillsides, past marshes, across moorland. They treated them like blocks of wood. Smashing, rubbing, polishing, they gave the rough slabs smooth surfaces, joints, chamfers, tenons; a ring of timber transformed into stone.

Over four thousand years ago people raised the great pillars, placed thick slabs across their tops, erected five even taller archways set like a horseshoe inside the circle. On stones at the exact east and south they carved impressions of a bronze dagger and axes, planned the ring to be in line with the midwinter sunset. The work took years, outlasting the people who began it. One marvels at their fanaticism. The accomplishment was astonishing; yet

Stonehenge, for all its amazement, is only one of more than a 1,000 prehistoric stone circles in Britain and Ireland. They tantalize with their mysteries.

Twenty-nine km north of Stonehenge is Avebury, a monster over a hundred times more spacious, its colossal stones bearing no art, standing in line with neither sun nor moon. It has no resemblance to Stonehenge and yet the rings share one grim reality. There were burials of women and children by the two entrances of Stonehenge, giving sanctity to the enclosure. A female dwarf was buried by Avebury's south entrance. Dozens of human jawbones lay in the surrounding ditch, perhaps fallen from scaffolds on which corpses had been exposed. Death was an intimate of stone circles, skeletons in central

Stonehenge. The curve of the neatly but laboriously carved lintels.

Avebury. Stones of the great south circle inside the earthwork.

graves, cremations lying in stone-slabbed cists. In ring after ring there were human bones, perhaps sacrifices offered to the powers of nature. The burnt bones of children were discovered in the middle of the Druids' Circle in north Wales. Fragments of children's skulls were found in a pit in the middle of Loanhead of Daviot in Aberdeenshire.

Bones were obvious. Subtleties were not. It was hardly two centuries ago that a sightline to the midsummer sunrise was first detected at Stonehenge. It was not until the 19th century that similar alignments were noticed in other stone circles. And it is only in the last decade that other orientations have been confirmed, unexpectedly to the cardinal points of north, east, south and west, directions that remain teasingly unexplained. How they were achieved in times when there was no Pole Star is unclear. Why they were created is debatable. What is apparent is that stone circles are far from the coarse rings of coarser stones that they have been termed in the past. It is only very slowly, with difficulty, that their secrets are being discovered. Wishful thinking has flourished, guesswork is plentiful , answers are rare.

Explanations for stone circles have differed over time. People in the Middle

vebury, Wiltshire (left).
Human remains have been found here, as in other stone circles.

he Heel Stone, Stonehenge (right), an outlying stone standing almost in line with the midsummer sunrise.

Ages thought the monstrous boulders had been put up by giants. By the 18th century giants were replaced by bloodstained druids dragging their victims to sacrificial altars. Druids disappeared. Victorians believed the rings were observatories for astronomer-priests scientifically examining the heavens. More recently and fancifully circles became centres of extra-sensory perception transmitted from ring to ring along precisely straight lines scores of kilometres long. Even more fantastically, circles were landing-pads for the flying saucers of explorers from outer space.

*S*tonehenge, as seen by the English
poet, artist and mystic, William
Blake, c.1815–20.

*S*tonehenge, from the historian
William Camden's **Britain**, 1610.

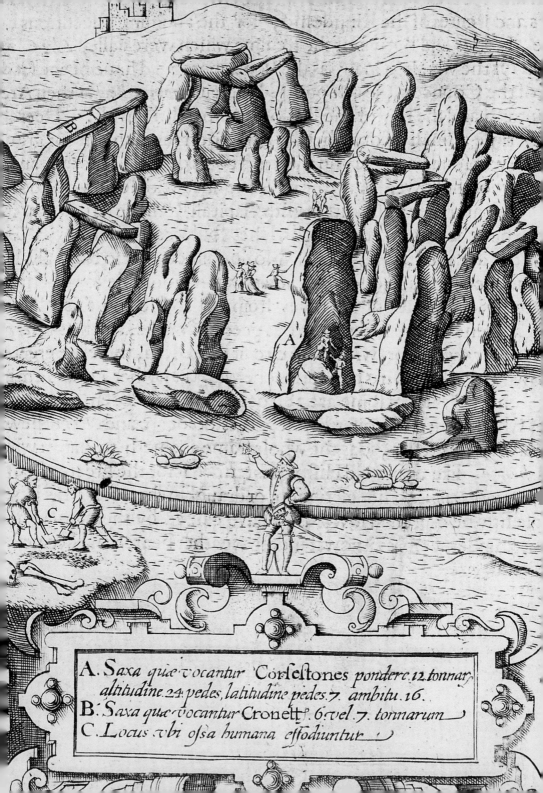

A. Saxa quæ vocantur Corseltones pondere 12. tonnar,
altitudine 24. pedes, latitudine pedes 7. ambitu 16.
B. Saxa quæ vocantur Cronett. 6. vel 7. tonnarum
C. Locus vbi ossa humana effodiuntur

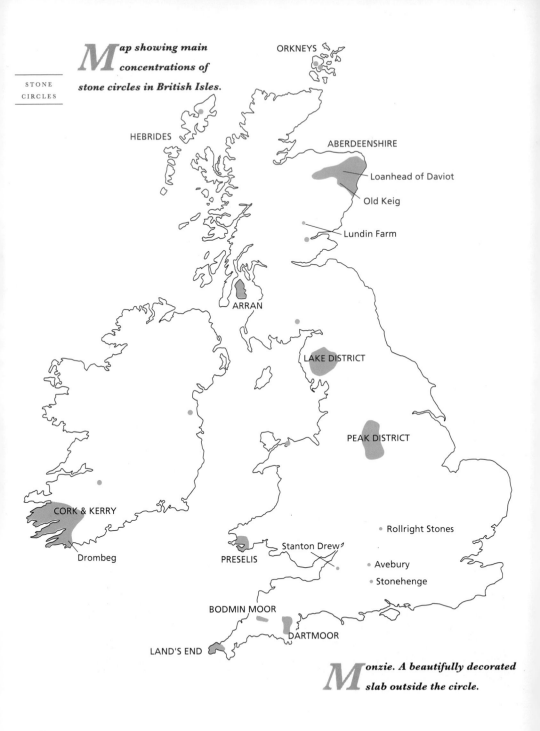

*M*ap showing main concentrations of stone circles in British Isles.

ORKNEYS

HEBRIDES

ABERDEENSHIRE

Loanhead of Daviot

Old Keig

Lundin Farm

ARRAN

LAKE DISTRICT

PEAK DISTRICT

CORK & KERRY

Rollright Stones

Drombeg

Stanton Drew

PRESELIS

Avebury

Stonehenge

BODMIN MOOR

LAND'S END

DARTMOOR

*M*onzie. A beautifully decorated slab outside the circle.

Circles, Stones and Styles

There were flickers, no more than flickers, of truth in some of this. The rest were delusions based upon ignorance. Reality was simpler. Wherever there were free-lying stones and good land for farming there were stone circles. They were erected by short-lived people (most men dying in their mid-thirties), women ten years younger, but they were energetic and enterprising, clearing forests with stone axes, opening wildernesses, putting up circles in the pioneered territories. The first rings were the handiwork of groups without metal. Later, with the discovery of copper and tin, others were put up by the followers of rich and powerful chieftains with murderous bronze daggers and axes. It is the misfortune and challenge for modern investigators that those people had no writing and no understandable art, as the strange depressions

and rings on the Monzie circle in Aberdeenshire show. Today we can see the stones they put up, we can recover the broken objects and the bones that they left, but these are the only clues to their needs and fears.

Adding to our problems, beliefs and customs were never identical. Even in the same region no ring was the same as another. Shapes were different, architecture and art were different, size was different. The Twelve Apostles in south-west Scotland could have accommodated 1,000 people but the shrunken Kirkhill a few miles away could hold no more than 20. There was no comprehensive blueprint for the design of a stone circle. Despite claims for geometrical layouts and of a national measure some 0.83 m long,

Midmar Kirk, Aberdeenshire (left). The packing-stones jammed under the recumbent stone still keep it horizontal.

Castlerigg near Keswick in the Lake District (right), one of the earliest stone circles.

adopted everywhere from the Shetlands down to Brittany, recent studies suggest that local measuring-rods, varying from community to community, are more probable.

Apart from Stonehenge, always the exception, the stones of every ring came from close by and were probably dragged on sledges by human muscle-power, levered and hauled upright into prepared holes, jammed tightly into place with stones, pebbles, clay, broken pottery – whatever was convenient. An average pillar weighed some four to six tonnes and could have been raised to the vertical by a score of labourers with the simplest of equipment: ropes, levers, antlers, and tools of wood, stone and flint. Other than the occasional shaping of the base of a stone to make its erection easier it was left in its natural state. It is noticeable, however, that it was the smoother, unweathered side that was chosen to face the interior of the circle.

Phases

Between 3300 and 900 BC there were three important phases of stone circle building. The earliest circles were erected in the centuries before 3000 BC on moors and hillsides around the coasts of the Irish Sea and northwards along the Irish–Scottish seaways. Rings like Castlerigg in the Lake District, Stenness in the Orkneys or Ballynoe in northern Ireland, were few but impressive. They were large, over 30 m across, stones closely set together, had

*R**ing of Brodgar, Orkney.***

*B**allynoe, Co. Down, Northern Ireland (above). Two later cairns were put up inside the circle.***

uncluttered centres, and were usually true circles. Some did have a flattened arc but this was possibly the slipshod result of a careless work-gang. Entrances to these splendid rings were marked by a wider gap and a pair of external portals. Outside some rings was a single standing stone, like a sign-post proclaiming that the land was occupied.

In the second phase, around 2600 BC, when metallurgy was introduced to the British Isles, many of the most perfect circles were constructed. Some

were enormous: giants like Stanton Drew, Somerset, or the Ring of Brodgar in the Orkneys were over 90 m in diameter. The majority, however, were much smaller, between 18 and 30 m in size. Although less grandiose they were intriguingly varied. There were circles and there were ovals whose longer axis was often set in line with a solar or lunar event. Numeracy is apparent. There was a regional tendency for a preferred number of stones whatever the length of the circumference, 12 in the Lake District, 13 in the

*Callanish,
Isle of Lewis.
A circle with a
centre stone
and radiating
rows.*

*D*own Tor, Dartmoor. A long
row of standing stones
leading uphill to the burial circle.

*G*rey Wethers, Dartmoor.
A pair of circles typical
of the south-west peninsula.

Hebrides, 4, 6 and 8 in central Scotland, 19 or 20 at Land's End, 5 in southern Ireland.

Styles also differed. There were plain rings. There were multiple sites, such as the paired Grey Wethers on Dartmoor and the three Hurlers on Bodmin Moor. There were concentric rings, rings with stones graded in height, rings with cobbled interiors. Central pillars were set up in Cornwall and in south-west Scotland and Ireland. Imposing avenues led to Avebury, Stanton Drew and Stonehenge. On Dartmoor rings were approached by long, meandering lines of standing stones. In the Peak District low stones stood in a rubble bank around a burial-cairn. In northern Scotland Cnoc an Liath-Bhaid, perhaps 'the stone of the grey prophet', is an outstanding oddity amongst these architectural eccentricities. On their steep hillside the stones were not put up in line along the perimeter of the ring but at right-angles across it, like the cogs of a mountain railway.

*G*ors Fawr,
Pembrokeshire,
lies beneath the
Preseli hills from
which the Stonehenge
bluestones came.

Recumbent Stone Circles

Of the many groups, one of the most informative about the customs and thinking of their makers is the recumbent stone circle tradition of Aberdeenshire. Densely concentrated in what seem to be family territories of 10.4 to 15.5 square km, and erected on chosen hill-terraces that provided long views

to the south, these rings – more than a hundred of them – had stones elegantly rising in height towards the south-west,

Old Keig, Aberdeenshire. The recumbent stone, 50 tonnes in weight, is perfectly horizontal.

where the tallest pair flanked a monstrous block lying on its side. Almost unbelievably, these gross, prostrate boulders were meticulously levelled. Even when as heavy as the 50-tonne monster at Old Keig, the vast slabs were so carefully levered, manoeuvred and set into position that even today their long, flat tops remain perfectly horizontal.

In front of them fragments of brilliantly glittering white quartz were scattered and this hints at the beliefs of those distant societies. Not only was burnt human bone deposited at the heart of the ring, but the moon was vital to the ceremonies. Small circular depressions known as cupmarks were ground out on pillars near the recumbent stone, or actually on it as at

Sunhoney, Aberdeenshire. The cupmarked recumbent stone was arranged to be in line with the southern moonset.

Sunhoney. The decorated standing stones were always in line with the moon, mainly at its setting. So was the recumbent, the southern moon sinking behind it, sometimes just where cupmarks had been carved. The broken quartz strewn against this 'lunar' block may have been visualized as bits of the moon itself, fallen from the heavenly body to which the dead went or from which life came.

*D*uloe, Cornwall.
*A circle unusually
composed of quartz blocks.*

This creates two mysteries. There are similar recumbent stone circles in south-western Ireland. Despite the hundreds of kilometres of land and sea between them the two areas share so many features – the recumbent stone, graded heights, two high pillars, internal burials and an emphasis upon the south-west – that it must be assumed that they were related through a movement of people and ideas. The Scottish circles are thought likely to be the earlier from the pottery found in them. In Ireland rings such as Drombeg

D rombeg recumbent stone circle, Co. Cork. The notch in the hills is in line with the midwinter sunset.

have been dated as late as 1000 BC, more than a thousand years after the first Scottish circles like Loanhead of Daviot.

The second mystery is the astronomy. Whereas the Scottish rings were aligned on the moon, the sites in Cork and Kerry were orientated on the sun – at Drombeg towards the midwinter sunset – an astronomical interest that implies that people had devised a solar calendar to record the time of seasonal gatherings. On such occasions offerings and supplications could be

made to the forces of nature that threatened societies with the otherwise uncontrollable disasters of storm, drought, famine and disease. Ignorant of scientific remedies the helplessness of the people was relieved by reliance on long-tried, seemingly successful rites.

The Decline of Stone Circles

By 2000 BC the tradition of building stone circles was in decline. In this final phase new rings were built in areas not previously settled. They were usually oval or distorted; they were tiny (some no more than 3 m across) and each region had its own character. In central Scotland ellipses of six or eight stones intermingled with sub-rectangular settings known as Four-Posters, Lundin Farm in Perthshire being a good example. In south-western Ireland in the counties of Cork and Kerry, the areas of recumbent stone circles, there were also five-stone counterparts of Scottish Four-Posters. They were squashed settings of four low boulders and an even lower recumbent, some

*L*undin Farm,
Perthshire (left).
A 'Four-Poster'
Scottish circle put up
on a burial mound.

*C*ircle 275, a tiny
'Irish' five-stone
ring on Penmaenmawr
in North Wales.

so reduced in size that they are often obscured by reeds and grass. They were so small, the stones so diminutive that they could comfortably have been dragged into position by the few members of isolated families in the green hills of Munster.

By 900 BC faith in the usefulness of stone circles had waned. In spite of repeated rituals, a persistent deterioration in the climate year after year convinced people that circles had lost their ability to control nature. Stonehenge was abandoned. Rings were left to decay. Iron Age communities ignored them. People in the Middle Ages avoided them as the work of the Devil. Victorian farmers removed stones for gateposts and walls. Misguided and always

disappointed treasure-hunters dug gaping pits. Indifference led to neglect and today some once-imposing rings are sadly misplaced. Sandy Road near Perth lies in an overgrown heather-bed on a housing estate. Tomnaverie recumbent stone circle in Aberdeenshire is perched above an encroaching quarry. Midmar Kirk in the same county is enclosed in a 19th-century churchyard. Ardblair in Perthshire has a road racing straight through it.

More positively, some circles have been rediscovered, like the one excavated by this writer on Machrie Moor, Arran, restored to the light after centuries of lying under peat. There have also been insights. Old ideas that the

Ballynoe, Co. Down. In the background are the Mountains of Mourne.

Duddo Four Stones, a reconstructed ring in Northumberland.

Machrie Moor XI, Arran. A stone circle, buried under peat, discovered in 1972 and later excavated by the author.

rings had been temples of the druids gave way to theories that they had been observatories for astronomer-priests. Today, more believably, they are considered to have been assembly places for seasonal gatherings whose occasions were established by sightlines to the sun or moon and whose strength was enhanced by bones of the dead. The discovery of such bones, traces of fires that once flamed inside the rings, trampled areas where participants had entered, maybe danced, even what the rings are called are clues to the ceremonies that once took place inside them.

*L*ong Meg,
Cumbria
(left), with
puzzling carvings
of rings, lines and
spirals on the
outlier.

*N*ine Stones,
Harthill,
Peak District.

Ceremony, Sex and Stonehenge

The names are like whispers from a fairy-tale: the Druid's Temple, Fingal's Cauldron, Athgreany, 'the field of the sun', Dans Maen, 'the stone dance'. Fairies are not entirely fanciful. Elva Plain in the Lake District derives from the Old Norse *elf-haugr*, 'the hill of elves'. At the most wraithlike level of folk-memory there are the Merry Maidens, the Trippet Stones, Long Meg and Her Daughters, the Nine Ladies, all of them recording how later people believed that the stones were girls petrified for dancing on the Sabbath. These may be Christian myths but the legends of dancing and music and young women are widespread from the Nine Maidens at Land's End to Haltadans, 'the limping dance' in the Shetlands, and across to Ireland at the Piper's Stones in Co. Wicklow. As rings of stones in other parts of the world were used for ritual dancing it is possible that the names of British rings preserve recollections of the activities that once took place inside them.

It is noticeable that it is always girls that are involved, never priests. Sometimes, as at The Weddings, three rings at Stanton Drew, it was the bride, groom and bawdily roistering guests that were turned into stone, as though there was a vague remembrance not only of music and dancing but of rites of fertility between men and women to ensure the fruitfulness of the land, acts of imitative magic that the Christian church condemned as obscene. People ignored the blasphemy. As late as this century childless wives stripped naked at the Rollright Stones near Oxford to rub themselves against the life-giving male pillars. Sexual activity within the rings is likely in prehistory. Lozenge-shaped and pillarlike stones opposite or against each other at Avebury and elsewhere have been interpreted as 'male' and 'female' symbolism as though affirming the need for fecundity in people, beasts, trees and crops.

Occasionally, the stones themselves were supposed to come to life, to dance at midnight, to search for a lost partner, or to wander down to a river or stream

*A*vebury. 'Male'
pillar and
'female' lozenge
stones in the Kennet
avenue.

*A*erial view of
Stonehenge,
showing the
earthworks beyond
the stones.

to drink, and the association with water is important. Avenues and rows often
led from a river to the circle as though water was essential to the ceremonies.

Stonehenge contains all the mysteries and some of the answers. In the
beginning, over five thousand years ago, it was an unimpressive circular
earthwork. It had two entrances. One, meticulously placed at the south, was

a narrow causeway across the ditch and through the bank. The other, wider, at the north-east, was in line with the most northerly rising of the moon. Standing beyond the enclosure was the famous outlying pillar of the Heel Stone, midway between the moon's major and minor risings.

There was a change of cult. Man-high bluestones from the Preseli mountains of Wales below which the Gors Fawr stone circle lies were erected in two intended concentric circles inside the earthwork. The north-eastern entrance was widened for its midpoint to be in line with the midsummer sunrise. Beyond it an earth-banked avenue stretched towards the River Avon. The project was rejected. Stonehenge was changed again.

*S**tonehenge. A view across the ditch from the little-known southern entrance.***

Preseli hills, where some of the stones for Stonehenge were quarried.

Around 2400 BC the bluestones were uprooted. They were replaced by the awesomely overbearing circle of lintelled pillars 5 m or more high. On the outer faces of three stones at the east axe-carvings were engraved. The axis was reversed. Dawn gave way to night. The horseshoe of archways inside the ring rose towards the south-west and the midwinter sunset. Inside the cramped centre of Stonehenge, where only a few of the élite could gather, stood the tall cylinder of the Altar Stone, likened to a phallic symbol. Outlines of weapons, a dagger and axes, were carved on a stone to the south and formalized outlines of a protectress of the dead were ground out on a pillar and a lintel to the west. A phallus carved of chalk was found near the stone. Sun, east, west, south, death and fertility all combined in the dark space at the heart of the ring, a space obscured from the unprivileged outside by the thick stones of the outer circle.

Almost three hundred brief generations have passed since the first stone circle was erected. Two thousand years have gone by since the last ring fell into disuse. Over long centuries the meanings of those sacred places were forgotten. It was a world alien to our thinking, a world in which human sacrifice may have been practised, a world dominated by the sun and moon and fear of the unexplained, a world of our forefathers whose works survive for us to admire, respect and struggle to understand.

Stonehenge. Carving of a dagger and an axe on Stone 53 south.

Stonehenge. Trilithon 53–4. The carvings are on Stone 53 on the left.

*J*ohn
Constable's
*Stonehenge, which
he wrote 'carries
you back . . . into
the obscurity of a
totally unknown
period'.
Watercolour,
exhibited 1836.*

STONE
CIRCLES

PHOTOGRAPHIC ACKNOWLEDGEMENTS
Cover Zefa; pp. 2–3, 4–5, 5 Aubrey Burl [AB];
p, 6 Michael Jenner [MJ]; p. 7 AB; p. 8 Fortean
Picture Library [FPL]; p. 9 e.t. archive;
pp. 11, 12, 13, 14 AB; pp. 14–15 Zefa;
pp. 16–17 MJ; pp. 18, 19 AB; pp. 20–21
FPL/Janet & Colin Bord [JCB]; pp. 22, 23 AB;
pp. 24–5 FPL/JCB;
pp. 26–7, 28, 29, 30t, 30b, 31, 32 AB;
p. 33 FPL/JCB; pp. 34t&b, 35, AB;
pp. 36, 37l FPL/JCB; p. 37r FPL;
pp. 38–9 e.t. archive/Victoria & Albert Museum.

First published in Great Britain 1997
by George Weidenfeld and Nicolson Ltd
The Orion Publishing Group
5 Upper St Martin's Lane
London WC2H 9EA

A CIP catalogue record for this book is available
from the British Library
ISBN 0 297 822721

Picture Research: Suzanne Williams

Design: Harry Green

Typeset in Baskerville